How to start

COARSE FISHING

a step-by-step guide

Text:
Liz French

Technical consultant:
Chris Turnbull

JARROLD

Other sports covered in this series are:

AMERICAN FOOTBALL   **SAILING A DINGHY**
BADMINTON   **SNOOKER**
BASKETBALL   **SOCCER**
BOWLS   **SQUASH**
CRICKET   **SWIMMING**
CROQUET   **TABLE TENNIS**
GET FIT FOR SPORT   **TENNIS**
GOLF   **WINDSURFING**
HOCKEY

How to start COARSE FISHING
ISBN 0-7117-0488-0

Text © Liz French 1991
This edition © Jarrold Publishing 1991
Illustrations by Chris Turnbull

First published 1991
Reprinted 1995

Designed and produced by
Parke Sutton Limited, Norwich
for Jarrold Publishing, Norwich
Printed in Great Britain 2/95

Contents

Introduction

As a newcomer to coarse fishing, you are certainly in good company. More than three million people enjoy angling at some level, whether as an occasional weekend pastime or as a passion pursued at every possible opportunity. It is, in fact, the most popular participant sport in the country, and it is easy to see why. Angling can be enjoyed equally by all age groups, and at different levels. Some fish purely for relaxation and the pleasure of the hours spent by the water; others specialise in a particular species and develop great expertise in the methods and skills needed to catch large specimens; others still enjoy the competitive side of the sport and take part in matches.

Whatever you want from angling, you'll need to understand some fundamental principles — and get yourself some basic tackle. This book will help you get going, with practical advice on the sort of tackle you'll need, where to find fish and how to identify the different species. You'll also find step-by-step instructions for the basic techniques and for handling fish as well as information on different baits. The terminology of angling can be a little confusing at first, so unfamiliar words and phrases are printed in *italics* as they appear in the book and are defined in the glossary on page 48.

A good first step for beginners is to join an angling club. Your local tackle shop, as well as being a good place to browse, pick up tips and talk to other enthusiasts, will also have a list of club secretaries in your area and will know which ones particularly welcome beginners. Your library may also be able to help, and should have details of any evening classes or other angling tuition schemes.

Most anglers are keen to share their knowledge and one of the very best ways to get started is to go fishing with someone who really knows what they're doing. Watching the experts in action, you will see that they have enormous respect for the fish and their habitat. You will also see that good fishing has very little to do with luck. But don't be daunted by the amount there is to learn. It is true that consistent success is only achieved through knowledge and skill, but that is the challenge of angling — and you will certainly have great fun learning!

GETTING STARTED

Seasons

The traditional fishing season runs from June 16th-March 14th inclusive. The Close Season was originally intended to give the fish peace and quiet whilst spawning, but has been relaxed in some areas, particularly on still waters. Ask your tackle dealer for full information about the seasons in specific waters.

Licences

Before you go fishing on any water, you'll need a rod licence. This is available from post offices throughout the country and will last you one complete season.

Shorter-term licences are also available — particularly useful if you only want to try the sport or are going fishing on holiday.

Permits and day-tickets

Some waters offer free fishing, others require a day or season ticket. In some cases you can buy the ticket at the site itself; others have to be bought in advance. Find out by:

● Visiting the venue — there will probably be a noticeboard telling you where you can get a day ticket if necessary.

● Asking at the tackle shop — some even sell permits themselves, but if not they will tell you who to approach.

● Checking in one of the 'Where to Fish' books available in good bookshops.

Joining clubs

Clubs manage the majority of waters in this country, and there are several advantages in joining one or more:

● Membership automatically gives you a permit for club waters at cheap rate.

● You get a chance to talk to experienced anglers and exchange information with other enthusiasts.

● Supporting clubs is good for angling in general — without them, a lot of good fishing sites would be lost.

Basic Kit

A quick browse round the tackle shop will reveal a staggering range of tackle, but you can actually get started with very little. This page shows the sort of kit you might aim for with a little experience. More detailed information on all the items is given in later sections.

Umbrella
To give shelter from wind and sun as well as rain. Pegs and guy ropes can be used to secure it in windy weather.

Leger rod (See page 8)

Specimen rod (See page 8)

Float rod (See page 8)

Holdall
Not essential, but certainly makes life a lot easier. A good rod holdall has compartments for several rods etc.

Float box
Foam rubber strips help keep your floats tidy and in good condition.

Tackle box (See page 10)
Many different types are available. May be made of wood, cane or fibreglass.

Bait box
Fitted with a lid and available in different sizes. A tightly lidded margarine tub makes a good bait carrier — punch holes in the lid for live bait (see pages 43-44).

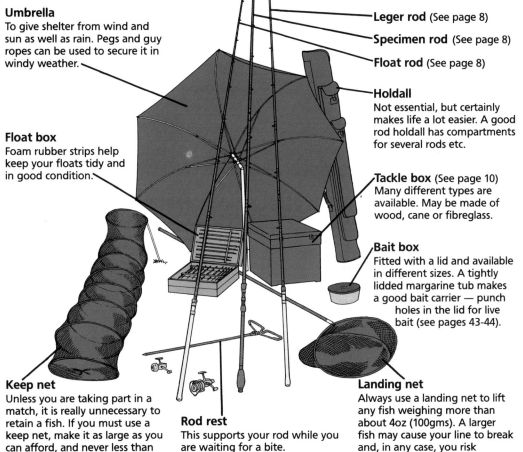

Keep net
Unless you are taking part in a match, it is really unnecessary to retain a fish. If you must use a keep net, make it as large as you can afford, and never less than 6ft (2m).

Rod rest
This supports your rod while you are waiting for a bite.

Landing net
Always use a landing net to lift any fish weighing more than about 4oz (100gms). A larger fish may cause your line to break and, in any case, you risk damaging the fish.

Rods

Coarse fishing can be divided into two types: *float fishing,* which uses a buoyant float to indicate bites (see pages 26 and 34); and *legering,* where the bait is anchored on the bed of the river or lake and a float is not used (pages 29 and 36). Different rods are used for each.

Float rods

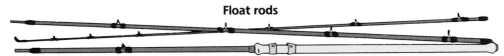

Float rods

Usually made of carbon fibre. The rod is divided into two or three sections. Lengths vary from 12-13ft (3.6-3.9m).

Rings, through which the line is threaded, are spaced at intervals along the line and are made from a variety of materials including stainless steel and silicon carbide. The latter is expensive but gives better performance.

Leger rods

Shorter than *float fishing* rods and usually made in two sections. Instead of a float, a leger weight is used, with a *swingtip* or *quivertip* to indicate bites. These may be built into the rod, but as a beginner your best choice is a 10ft (3m) legering rod with a *tipring* screw fitting which accommodates either.

Specimen rods

11-12ft (3.3m) long and stronger, for casting heavier weights and catching bigger fish.

Leger rods

Hint box: choosing a rod

Go to a good tackle dealer — preferably mid-week when the shop is less busy. Take someone who knows about fishing.

DO choose:

- The best rod you can afford.
- Carbon fibre.
- The longest rod you can handle*.
- A rod with a good number of rings.

DON'T choose:

- Rods labelled 'junior'.
- A short solid fibreglass rod.
- A bright painted rod.
- A wooden or plastic handled rod.

*Very young anglers can buy a leger rod and use it for float fishing until they are bigger — better than getting an inferior, short rod they'll grow out of.

Reels

There are numerous types of reel available but as a beginner your best choice is a fixed spool reel. These are either open-faced (you can see the line on the spool) or closed-face.

Open-faced reel

- A very versatile reel: the most popular for coarse fishing.
- Allows accurate casting over long distances.
- *Slipping clutch* mechanism adjusts according to strength of line.

Closed-face reel

- Good control for *trotting*.
- Accurate casting over longer distances not so easy.

Hint box: choosing a reel

Do go for a reputable make with spares and repairs available. It's worth getting the best you can afford — cheap reels may look the same but are made of inferior materials and won't last well. Choose one with two spools if possible — one for lighter and one for heavier lines.

Check that:

- The reel turns smoothly, even at speed.
- The reel is suitable for you if you are left-handed.

- The *bale arm* opens and closes smoothly.
- The *slipping clutch* works smoothly.

Inside the Tackle Box

Here's what your tackle box might contain . . .

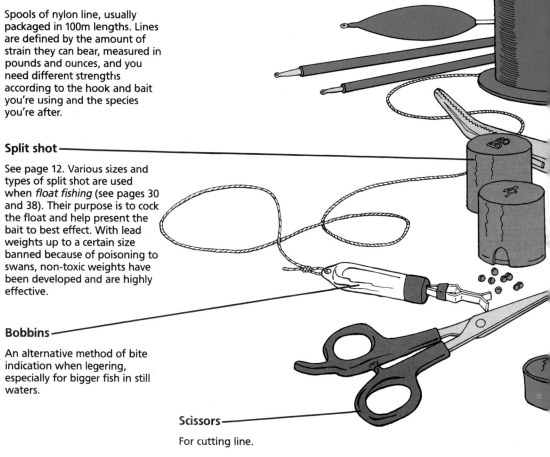

Line

Spools of nylon line, usually packaged in 100m lengths. Lines are defined by the amount of strain they can bear, measured in pounds and ounces, and you need different strengths according to the hook and bait you're using and the species you're after.

Split shot

See page 12. Various sizes and types of split shot are used when *float fishing* (see pages 30 and 38). Their purpose is to cock the float and help present the bait to best effect. With lead weights up to a certain size banned because of poisoning to swans, non-toxic weights have been developed and are highly effective.

Bobbins

An alternative method of bite indication when legering, especially for bigger fish in still waters.

Scissors

For cutting line.

Floats

Various floats are used for *float fishing* according to the habitat and species. See pages 30-31 and 38-39.

Hook tyer gadget

Invaluable for tying on spade end hooks (see page 12).

Hooks

See page 12. Hooks are numbered from 2-26 in even numbers according to size, 2 being the largest. The size you use depends on the bait and the target species. Hooks can be bought ready tied to line, but it is better to learn to tie your own (see page 13).

Forceps

A useful item for removing hooks.

Hook disgorger

For removing hooks — a vital item for your box.

Leger weights

For most legering methods, the Arlesey *bomb* is the only weight you'll need. It is available in a variety of sizes from $\frac{1}{4}$oz to around 4oz (7-100gms).

Float bands

Flexible rubber tubing of various widths used to hold floats in place on the line.

Hooks and Weights

Hooks

A wide variety is available.
Parts of the hook:

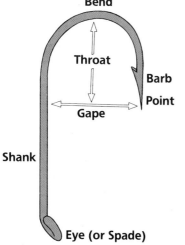

Forged hooks are much stronger and the shank is flat in cross-section.

Sizes

Size varies from the tiny 26 to the large 2. Those shown are actual size.

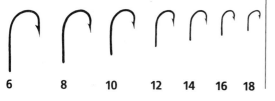

Weights

Split shot

For cocking the float in *float fishing*.
Identified according to size, from the smallest no. 10 to the SSG. You can buy a pack of split shot all one size, or in a segmented dispenser containing a selection of sizes.

Leger weights

For legering, you'll need a selection of Arlesey *bombs* ranging in size from about ½oz to 1oz (12-25gms) though they are available in weights up to about 4oz (100 gms).

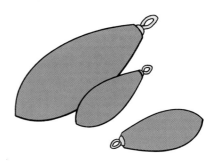

Knots

You'll need to know a few basic knots for tying on hooks and for attaching a hooklength to the reel line. Always wet the line (lick it!) before tightening, and give it a steady, firm pull, not a quick tug.

Blood knot

A good knot for securing the hooklength to the reel line if they are of similar thickness.

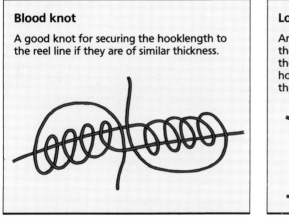

Loop to loop

Another way of attaching the hooklength to the main line. First make a loop in the end of the reel line and another at one end of the hooklength. Then thread the free end through both loops and pull.

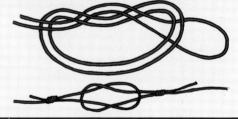

Blood knot for eyed hooks

Passing the line through the eye twice gives a much more secure knot.

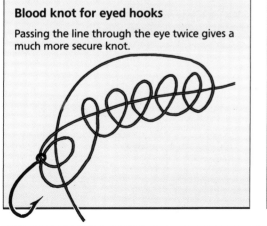

Knot for spade end hooks

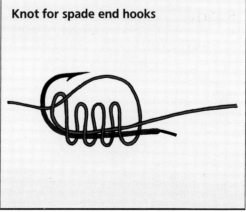

THE SPECIES

This section gives you basic information on the most commonly caught coarse fish. The different habitats, baits and techniques referred to are described in more detail in later sections of the book.

Identifying Fish

Colour is the most important clue, though it can vary according to size, age and habitat of the fish, and may be different for a dead specimen.

So look at the colour in conjunction with the body shape, fin position and scales. Weight and measurement are also useful clues. You'll find two weights given here for each fish: the first is an average adult fish, the second is what to aim for if you're after a really good specimen.

External features of a fish

It's a good idea to know from the start what a fish looks like!

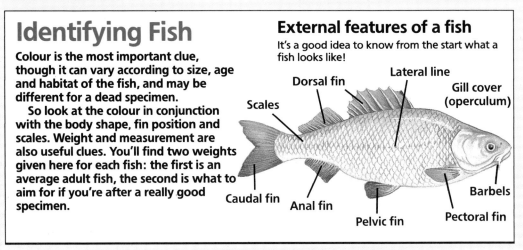

Dorsal fin · Lateral line · Gill cover (operculum) · Scales · Barbels · Caudal fin · Anal fin · Pelvic fin · Pectoral fin

Roach

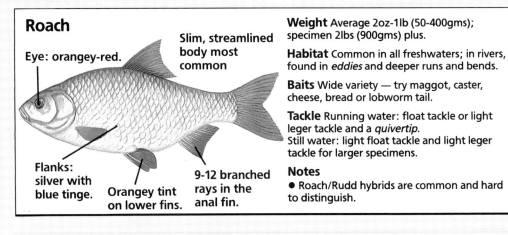

Eye: orangey-red.

Slim, streamlined body most common

Flanks: silver with blue tinge.

Orangey tint on lower fins.

9-12 branched rays in the anal fin.

Weight Average 2oz-1lb (50-400gms); specimen 2lbs (900gms) plus.

Habitat Common in all freshwaters; in rivers, found in *eddies* and deeper runs and bends.

Baits Wide variety — try maggot, caster, cheese, bread or lobworm tail.

Tackle Running water: float tackle or light leger tackle and a *quivertip*.
Still water: light float tackle and light leger tackle for larger specimens.

Notes
● Roach/Rudd hybrids are common and hard to distinguish.

Rudd

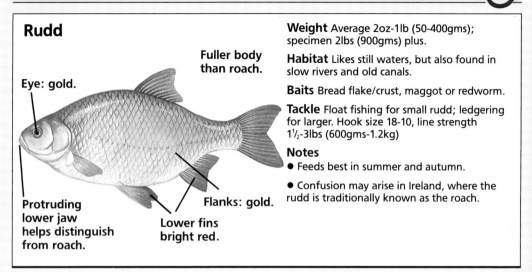

Fuller body than roach.

Eye: gold.

Protruding lower jaw helps distinguish from roach.

Flanks: gold.

Lower fins bright red.

Weight Average 2oz-1lb (50-400gms); specimen 2lbs (900gms) plus.

Habitat Likes still waters, but also found in slow rivers and old canals.

Baits Bread flake/crust, maggot or redworm.

Tackle Float fishing for small rudd; ledgering for larger. Hook size 18-10, line strength 1½-3lbs (600gms-1.2kg)

Notes
● Feeds best in summer and autumn.

● Confusion may arise in Ireland, where the rudd is traditionally known as the roach.

Bream

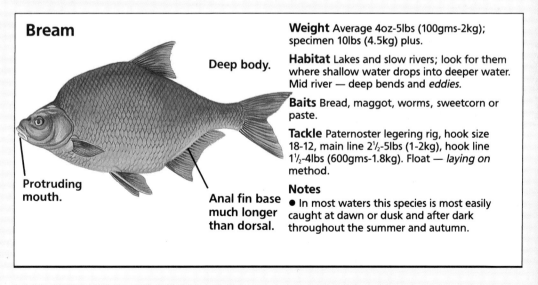

Deep body.

Protruding mouth.

Anal fin base much longer than dorsal.

Weight Average 4oz-5lbs (100gms-2kg); specimen 10lbs (4.5kg) plus.

Habitat Lakes and slow rivers; look for them where shallow water drops into deeper water. Mid river — deep bends and *eddies*.

Baits Bread, maggot, worms, sweetcorn or paste.

Tackle Paternoster legering rig, hook size 18-12, main line 2½-5lbs (1-2kg), hook line 1½-4lbs (600gms-1.8kg). Float — *laying on* method.

Notes
● In most waters this species is most easily caught at dawn or dusk and after dark throughout the summer and autumn.

Dace

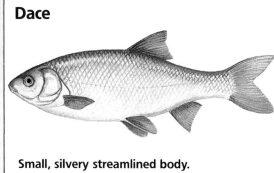

Small, silvery streamlined body.

Weight Average 1-6oz (30gms-170gms); specimen 1lb (450gms).

Habitat Clean streamy rivers.

Baits Maggots, hemps, casters.

Tackle Float trotting — stick float or waggler. Hook size 20-14; main line 2½lbs (1kg), hook line 1-1½lbs (400-600gms).

Notes
● Easy to mistake for small chub: only distinguishable by concave, clear fins.

'King' Carp: Common, Leather and Mirror

These are cultivated carp, with rounder, deeper bodies than the wild carp. Their habitats include large lakes and gravel pits. Baits and tackle are the same as for the wild carp.

Barbels

1 Common Carp

Weight Average 2-15lbs (900gms-6.8kg); specimen 20lbs (9kg).

2 Mirror Carp

Rows or groups of very large scales.

Weight Average 2-15lbs (900gms-6.8kg); specimen 20lbs (9kg).

3 Leather Carp

Hardly any scales.

Weight Average 2-15lbs (900gms-6.8kg); specimen 20lbs (9kg).

Wild Carp

Body colour varies: top of body and head usually brown-grey.

Slimmish body.

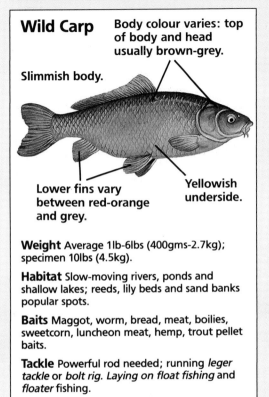

Lower fins vary between red-orange and grey.

Yellowish underside.

Weight Average 1lb-6lbs (400gms-2.7kg); specimen 10lbs (4.5kg).

Habitat Slow-moving rivers, ponds and shallow lakes; reeds, lily beds and sand banks popular spots.

Baits Maggot, worm, bread, meat, boilies, sweetcorn, luncheon meat, hemp, trout pellet baits.

Tackle Powerful rod needed; running *leger tackle* or *bolt rig*. Laying on float fishing and *floater* fishing.

Notes

● Although smaller than the cultivated species, the wild carp is a faster, harder-fighting fish.

● Mostly a summer species, though can be caught in winter.

● Feeds best at dawn, dusk and night in summer; also on the surface in bright sunlight.

Crucian Carp

Colour: golden-bronze.

Quite similar to common carp but no *barbels*.

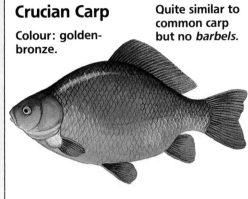

Weight Average 4oz-1lb (100-400gms); (900gms).

Habitat Swampy pools; estate lakes; farm ponds. Very tolerant of pollution and low oxygen content in water.

Baits Bread flakes, maggots, redworms, boilies, sweetcorn.

Tackle Float fishing — laying on or *lift* methods. Hook size 16-10; line 1½-3lbs (600gms-1.2kg)

Notes

● Very much a summer species — seldom caught in winter. Feeds best at dawn and dusk and at night.

● Smaller but hardier than other carp. Not found in Scotland or Ireland and not common in Wales or the north of England.

● Crucian/common carp *hybrids* are not uncommon. Check for the presence of mouth *barbels* if unsure: hybrids may have one but not both.

Tench

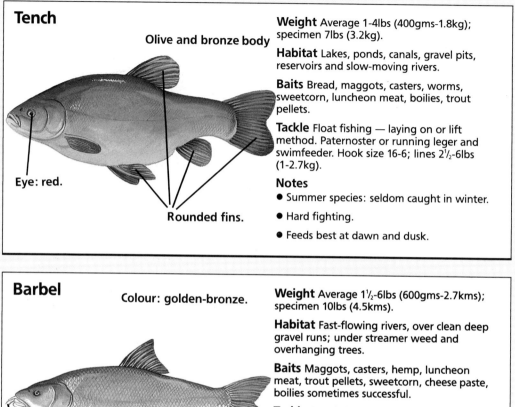

Olive and bronze body

Eye: red.

Rounded fins.

Weight Average 1-4lbs (400gms-1.8kg); specimen 7lbs (3.2kg).

Habitat Lakes, ponds, canals, gravel pits, reservoirs and slow-moving rivers.

Baits Bread, maggots, casters, worms, sweetcorn, luncheon meat, boilies, trout pellets.

Tackle Float fishing — laying on or lift method. Paternoster or running leger and swimfeeder. Hook size 16-6; lines $2\frac{1}{2}$-6lbs (1-2.7kg).

Notes
● Summer species: seldom caught in winter.
● Hard fighting.
● Feeds best at dawn and dusk.

Barbel

Colour: golden-bronze.

Four long *barbels* on mouth

Orange pectoral, pelvic and anal fins.

Weight Average $1\frac{1}{2}$-6lbs (600gms-2.7kms); specimen 10lbs (4.5kms).

Habitat Fast-flowing rivers, over clean deep gravel runs; under streamer weed and overhanging trees.

Baits Maggots, casters, hemp, luncheon meat, trout pellets, sweetcorn, cheese paste, boilies sometimes successful.

Tackle Mostly legering and swimfeeders. Strong rod and lines. Hooks 16-6; line 4-8lbs (1.8-3.6kms).

Notes
● Feeds best during summer and autumn, especially at dusk and in the dark.

● Also caught in mild weather during winter, when the river is fining down after flooding.

Chub

Torpedo shaped.

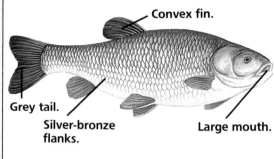

Convex fin.

Grey tail.

Silver-bronze flanks.

Large mouth.

Weight Average 1-3lbs (400gms-1.2kgs); specimen 5lbs (2kgs).

Habitat Rivers, streams and some gravel pits.

Baits Maggots, casters, bread, worms, sweetcorn, hemp and tares, trout pellets, luncheon meat, cheese paste. Boilies are sometimes successful.

Tackle Float or leger; hooks 16-6; line 2½-5lbs (1-2.3kgs).

Notes
● Very shy fish which will feed in almost any conditions all year round.

Perch

Large head.

Spiked dorsal fin.

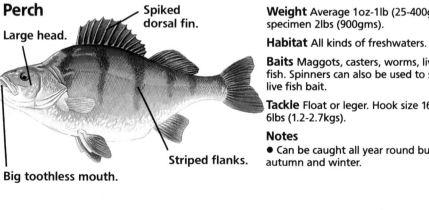

Striped flanks.

Big toothless mouth.

Weight Average 1oz-1lb (25-400gms); specimen 2lbs (900gms).

Habitat All kinds of freshwaters.

Baits Maggots, casters, worms, live and dead fish. Spinners can also be used to simulate a live fish bait.

Tackle Float or leger. Hook size 16-6; line 3-6lbs (1.2-2.7kgs).

Notes
● Can be caught all year round but best in autumn and winter.

Pike

Our biggest native predator.

**Torpedo shaped
with mottled
green flanks.**

Weight Average 1-14lbs (400gms-6.3kgs);
specimen 20lbs (9kgs) plus — and record over
45lbs (20kgs).

Habitat Lakes, rivers, reservoirs, gravel pits,
locks.

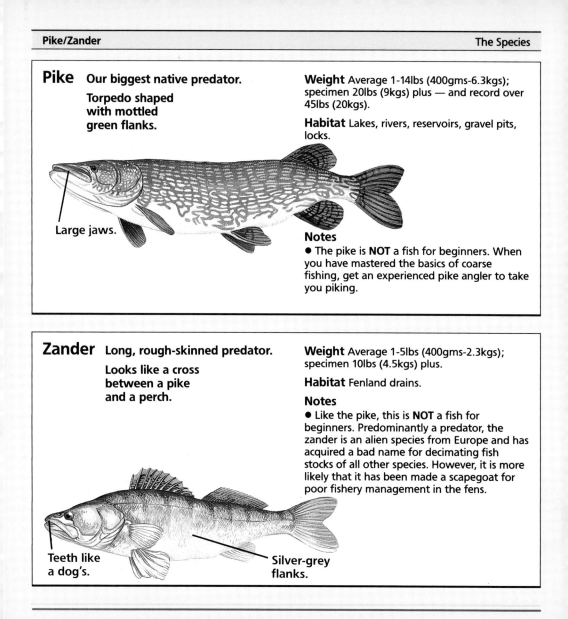

Large jaws.

Notes
● The pike is **NOT** a fish for beginners. When
you have mastered the basics of coarse
fishing, get an experienced pike angler to take
you piking.

Zander

Long, rough-skinned predator.

**Looks like a cross
between a pike
and a perch.**

Weight Average 1-5lbs (400gms-2.3kgs);
specimen 10lbs (4.5kgs) plus.

Habitat Fenland drains.

Notes
● Like the pike, this is **NOT** a fish for
beginners. Predominantly a predator, the
zander is an alien species from Europe and has
acquired a bad name for decimating fish
stocks of all other species. However, it is more
likely that it has been made a scapegoat for
poor fishery management in the fens.

Teeth like
a dog's.

Silver-grey
flanks.

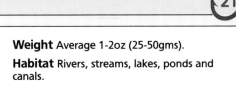
Gudgeon

Small, grey-brown.

Weight Average 1-2oz (25-50gms).

Habitat Rivers, streams, lakes, ponds and canals.

Baits Maggots and bloodworm.

Tackle Light *float fishing* best; can also be caught on a light leger.

Notes
- Popular fish with *match anglers*.

Large head, protractile mouth and barbels.

Eel Long snake-like fish which migrates to the Sargasso Sea to breed.

Weight Average 6oz-1½lbs (150-600gms); specimen 5lbs (2.3kgs).

Habitat Rivers, lakes, ponds, canals and estuaries.

Baits Worms and fish.

Tackle Strong specimen rod, 10lb (4.5kgs) line, wire traces and size 4 or 2 hook.

Notes
- **NOT** a fish for beginners.

- Feeds best during spring and summer when dark.

- Some counties allow eel fishing during the close season.

GENERAL SKILLS

Get the basic skills right from the start and you will save yourself time and trouble later.

Setting Up

Before you even leave home, you should:
● Check you are sensibly dressed. Best to wear lots of layers you can peel off if necessary. Wellingtons or waders are a good idea.

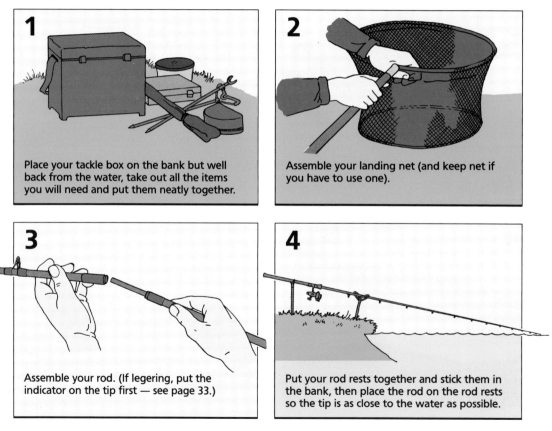

1 Place your tackle box on the bank but well back from the water, take out all the items you will need and put them neatly together.

2 Assemble your landing net (and keep net if you have to use one).

3 Assemble your rod. (If legering, put the indicator on the tip first — see page 33.)

4 Put your rod rests together and stick them in the bank, then place the rod on the rod rests so the tip is as close to the water as possible.

● Check, too, that you've got all the tackle and bait you need. **NEVER go out without a hook** *disgorger.*

● Once you get to the place you are fishing, take time to choose your *swim* carefully (see pages 24-25 and 32-33) and then set up.

● Doing this methodically will avoid getting in a mess and losing or damaging equipment.

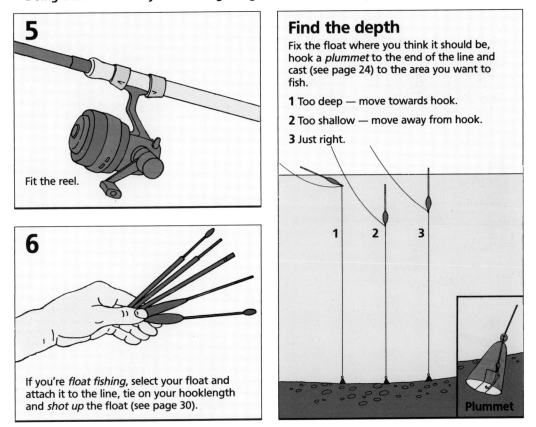

5

Fit the reel.

6

If you're *float fishing*, select your float and attach it to the line, tie on your hooklength and *shot up* the float (see page 30).

Find the depth

Fix the float where you think it should be, hook a *plummet* to the end of the line and cast (see page 24) to the area you want to fish.

1 Too deep — move towards hook.

2 Too shallow — move away from hook.

3 Just right.

1   2   3

Plummet

Casting

Once you're set up, the next step is to hook your bait (see pages 42-47) and then you are ready to cast.

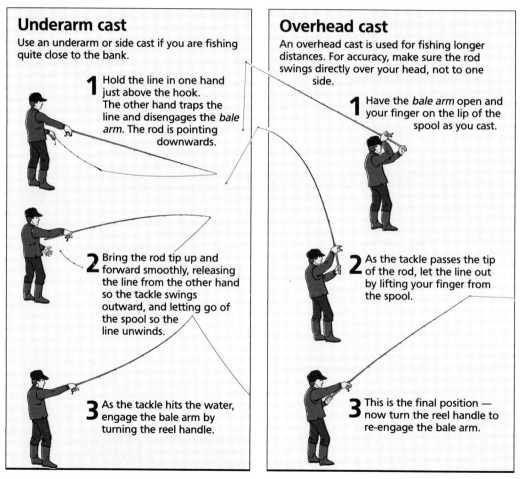

Underarm cast

Use an underarm or side cast if you are fishing quite close to the bank.

1 Hold the line in one hand just above the hook. The other hand traps the line and disengages the *bale arm*. The rod is pointing downwards.

2 Bring the rod tip up and forward smoothly, releasing the line from the other hand so the tackle swings outward, and letting go of the spool so the line unwinds.

3 As the tackle hits the water, engage the bale arm by turning the reel handle.

Overhead cast

An overhead cast is used for fishing longer distances. For accuracy, make sure the rod swings directly over your head, not to one side.

1 Have the *bale arm* open and your finger on the lip of the spool as you cast.

2 As the tackle passes the tip of the rod, let the line out by lifting your finger from the spool.

3 This is the final position — now turn the reel handle to re-engage the bale arm.

Striking and Playing

Getting a bite is always exciting, but knowing what to do next is vital if you don't want to lose the fish.

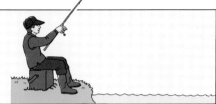

Striking

When a bite is indicated, pull your rod quickly but smoothly upwards or sideways until you feel the fish. **Then stop** — or you'll probably snap your hookline. Keep the rod well up to stay in contact with the fish.

Playing

This means keeping control of the fish as it fights to get away. Playing skills come with practice and experience, so don't expect to land every fish you hook. A few basic guidelines will, however, help you avoid some common mistakes.

There are two effective but distinctly different ways of playing fish.

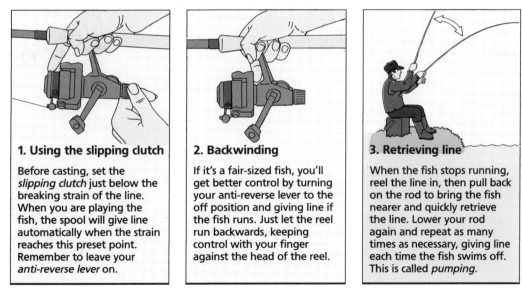

1. Using the slipping clutch

Before casting, set the *slipping clutch* just below the breaking strain of the line. When you are playing the fish, the spool will give line automatically when the strain reaches this preset point. Remember to leave your *anti-reverse lever* on.

2. Backwinding

If it's a fair-sized fish, you'll get better control by turning your anti-reverse lever to the off position and giving line if the fish runs. Just let the reel run backwards, keeping control with your finger against the head of the reel.

3. Retrieving line

When the fish stops running, reel the line in, then pull back on the rod to bring the fish nearer and quickly retrieve the line. Lower your rod again and repeat as many times as necessary, giving line each time the fish swims off. This is called *pumping*.

Landing

Many fish get away at this stage. The first thing to remember is to take your time: don't try to rush the fish into the net or you'll probably lose it. The second important point is always to bring the fish to the net, NEVER the net to the fish.

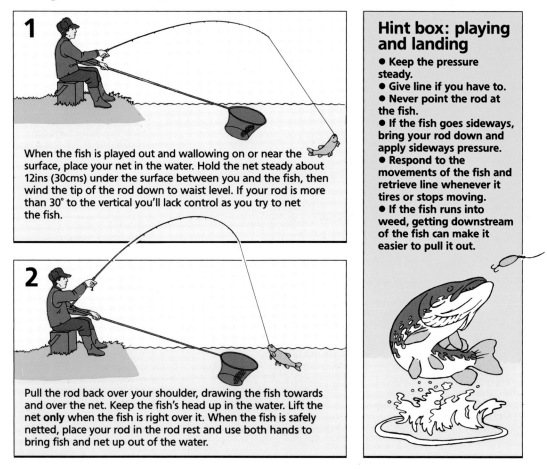

1

When the fish is played out and wallowing on or near the surface, place your net in the water. Hold the net steady about 12ins (30cms) under the surface between you and the fish, then wind the tip of the rod down to waist level. If your rod is more than 30° to the vertical you'll lack control as you try to net the fish.

2

Pull the rod back over your shoulder, drawing the fish towards and over the net. Keep the fish's head up in the water. Lift the net **only** when the fish is right over it. When the fish is safely netted, place your rod in the rod rest and use both hands to bring fish and net up out of the water.

Hint box: playing and landing

● Keep the pressure steady.
● Give line if you have to.
● Never point the rod at the fish.
● If the fish goes sideways, bring your rod down and apply sideways pressure.
● Respond to the movements of the fish and retrieve line whenever it tires or stops moving.
● If the fish runs into weed, getting downstream of the fish can make it easier to pull it out.

Handling Fish

Always handle fish carefully and gently, and never retain them any longer than necessary.

Removing hooks

1

Wet your hands and hold the fish gently but firmly just behind the gill openings. If the hook is near the front of its mouth, you can carefully remove it with your fingers or forceps.

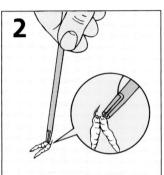

2

If the hook is further back, or deeply embedded, use your *disgorger*.

3

It's easier to leave a larger fish in the net while you remove the hook.

Weighing and photographing

4

This is the correct way to hold a fish for photographing. It is well supported, with wet hands, and there is very little pressure on the gills or body.

5

Weigh a fish in a wet knotless mesh bag or sling.

6

To return fish, gently gather up the keep net until you get to the fish, then put the mouth of the net underwater and let them swim out.

STILL WATER FISHING

Locating Fish: Lakes and Ponds

Fish are seldom found randomly or evenly dotted around a fishery. So when you go fishing, your first job is to find the likeliest spot for catching them. With experience you will develop an understanding of fish behaviour and get to know how and where to locate them even in unfamiliar waters. These diagrams will give you some general practical pointers.

An old-established lake produced by damming a stream and flooding the valley.

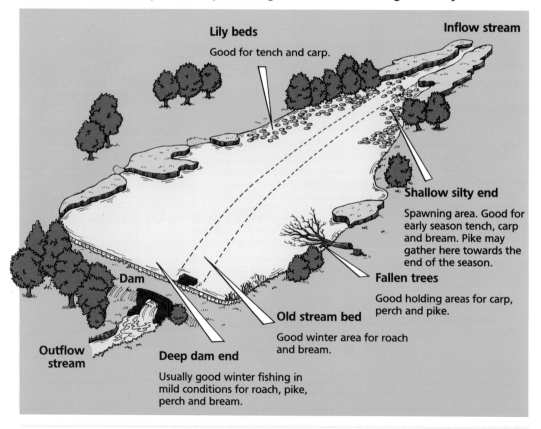

Lily beds
Good for tench and carp.

Inflow stream

Shallow silty end
Spawning area. Good for early season tench, carp and bream. Pike may gather here towards the end of the season.

Dam

Fallen trees
Good holding areas for carp, perch and pike.

Old stream bed
Good winter area for roach and bream.

Outflow stream

Deep dam end
Usually good winter fishing in mild conditions for roach, pike, perch and bream.

Locating Fish: Gravel Pits

There are numerous flooded gravel workings throughout the country, many of them superb fisheries, especially for bigger specimens.

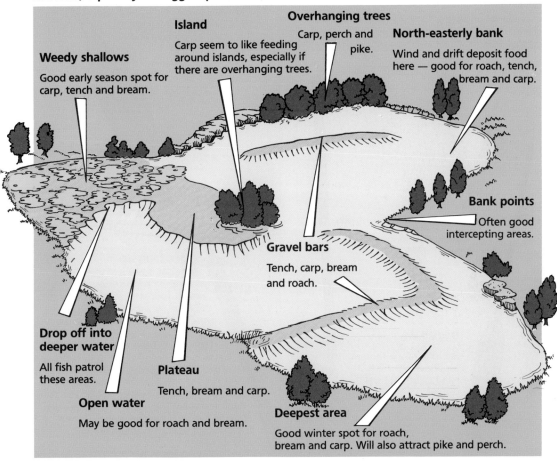

Overhanging trees

Carp, perch and pike.

Island

Carp seem to like feeding around islands, especially if there are overhanging trees.

North-easterly bank

Wind and drift deposit food here — good for roach, tench, bream and carp.

Weedy shallows

Good early season spot for carp, tench and bream.

Bank points

Often good intercepting areas.

Gravel bars

Tench, carp, bream and roach.

Drop off into deeper water

All fish patrol these areas.

Plateau

Tench, bream and carp.

Open water

May be good for roach and bream.

Deepest area

Good winter spot for roach, bream and carp. Will also attract pike and perch.

Float Fishing Methods

This section shows you the basic set-ups for *float fishing* in still waters.

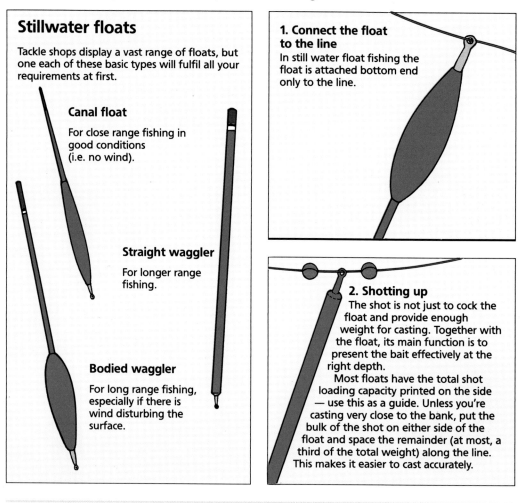

Stillwater floats

Tackle shops display a vast range of floats, but one each of these basic types will fulfil all your requirements at first.

Canal float

For close range fishing in good conditions (i.e. no wind).

Straight waggler

For longer range fishing.

Bodied waggler

For long range fishing, especially if there is wind disturbing the surface.

1. Connect the float to the line

In still water float fishing the float is attached bottom end only to the line.

2. Shotting up

The shot is not just to cock the float and provide enough weight for casting. Together with the float, its main function is to present the bait effectively at the right depth.

Most floats have the total shot loading capacity printed on the side — use this as a guide. Unless you're casting very close to the bank, put the bulk of the shot on either side of the float and space the remainder (at most, a third of the total weight) along the line. This makes it easier to cast accurately.

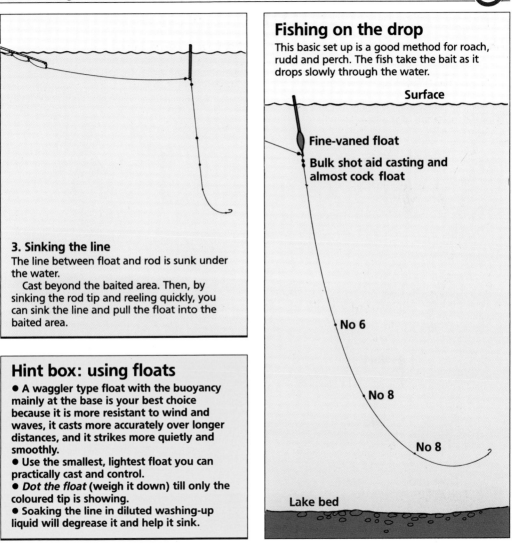

3. Sinking the line

The line between float and rod is sunk under the water.

Cast beyond the baited area. Then, by sinking the rod tip and reeling quickly, you can sink the line and pull the float into the baited area.

Hint box: using floats

● A waggler type float with the buoyancy mainly at the base is your best choice because it is more resistant to wind and waves, it casts more accurately over longer distances, and it strikes more quietly and smoothly.
● Use the smallest, lightest float you can practically cast and control.
● *Dot the float* (weigh it down) till only the coloured tip is showing.
● Soaking the line in diluted washing-up liquid will degrease it and help it sink.

Fishing on the drop

This basic set up is a good method for roach, rudd and perch. The fish take the bait as it drops slowly through the water.

Surface

Fine-vaned float

Bulk shot aid casting and almost cock float

No 6

No 8

No 8

Lake bed

Laying on

This is a good method for bream, tench, crucian carp, roach and perch. The bottom shot is set a short distance above the hook and lies on the bottom with the bait. A fish can take the bait without feeling the weight of the shot, but the float will give you a very obvious indication of the bite.

Lift method

When the fish picks up the bait it also lifts the SSG shot, so the float pops to the surface. A good method for tench, carp, bream and crucian carp.

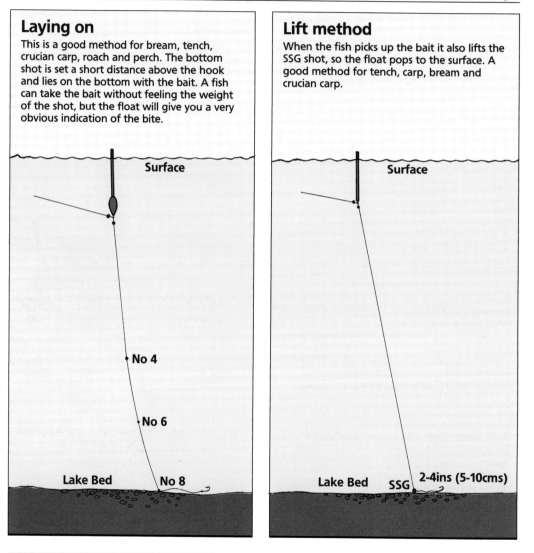

Surface

No 4

No 6

Lake Bed   No 8

Surface

Lake Bed   SSG 2-4ins (5-10cms)

Legering Methods

Here the bait is anchored to the bottom without the use of a float. Legering allows you to fish on the bottom in deeper water than with a float; the heavier weight also allows longer casting. There are many different legering methods; the following pages show you some of the most useful for still water fishing.

Bite indication

There are several ways of detecting a bite when legering.

1. Swingtip

Very good for sensitive detection of delicate bites. After casting, set the rod on two rests and tighten the line up until the *swingtip* rests at a slight angle. A bite will make the tip pull up or drop back.

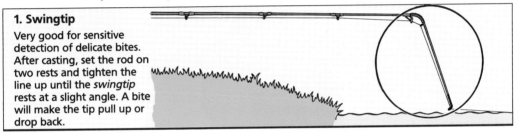

2. Bobbin

Good for bold biting fish, usually big roach, tench or bream, and sometimes perch. After casting, tighten up to the weight. Put the rod on the rest and clip the *bobbin* on between the reel and the first eye so that it hangs down in a 'V' under the rod. Bites will make the bobbin either lift or fall. Bobbins can be used in conjunction with an *electric bite indicator.*

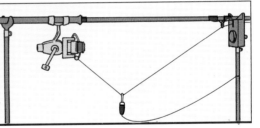

3. Monkey climber

A useful gadget in windy conditions especially when used with a *bolt rig* for carp and tench (see page 35).

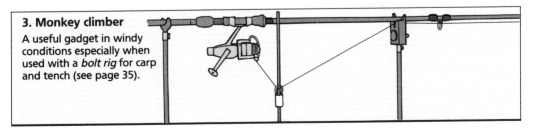

Basic legering rigs for still waters

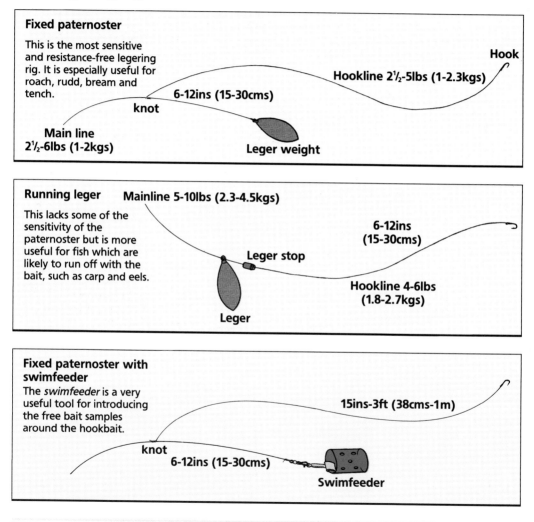

Fixed paternoster

This is the most sensitive and resistance-free legering rig. It is especially useful for roach, rudd, bream and tench.

Hook

Hookline 2½-5lbs (1-2.3kgs)

6-12ins (15-30cms)

knot

Main line 2½-6lbs (1-2kgs)

Leger weight

Running leger

Mainline 5-10lbs (2.3-4.5kgs)

This lacks some of the sensitivity of the paternoster but is more useful for fish which are likely to run off with the bait, such as carp and eels.

Leger stop

6-12ins (15-30cms)

Hookline 4-6lbs (1.8-2.7kgs)

Leger

Fixed paternoster with swimfeeder

The *swimfeeder* is a very useful tool for introducing the free bait samples around the hookbait.

15ins-3ft (38cms-1m)

knot

6-12ins (15-30cms)

Swimfeeder

Carp bolt rig

Boilies (see page 46) can be fished for carp by using a bolt rig. It is designed to create maximum resistance which will panic the carp into bolting after picking up the bait, thus setting the hook. Being too hard to fix effectively straight onto the hook, boilies are fixed onto a *hair rig*. This makes it more difficult for the fish to reject the bait without hooking itself.

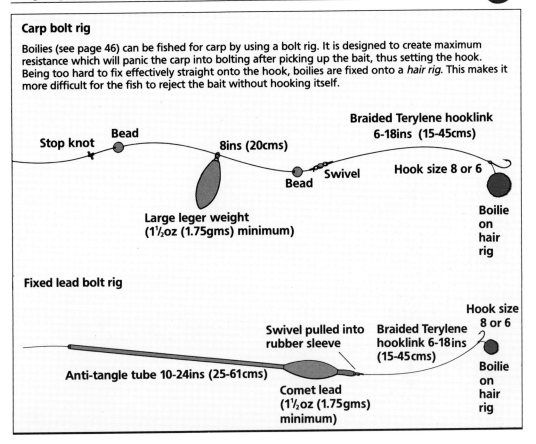

Braided Terylene hooklink 6-18ins (15-45cms)

Stop knot **Bead** **8ins (20cms)**

Bead **Swivel** **Hook size 8 or 6**

Large leger weight (1½oz (1.75gms) minimum)

Boilie on hair rig

Fixed lead bolt rig

Anti-tangle tube 10-24ins (25-61cms)

Swivel pulled into rubber sleeve **Braided Terylene hooklink 6-18ins (15-45cms)** **Hook size 8 or 6**

Comet lead (1½oz (1.75gms) minimum)

Boilie on hair rig

Hint box: legering
● Always cast to the same area — pick the reflection of an object on the far bank, and always cast to that.
● While confident fish will give bold bites on short *hooklinks*, shyer fish will need longer hooklinks to allow them to build up confidence.

RIVER FISHING

Locating Fish: Rivers

Different species like different areas in a river. By learning to identify these different habitat preferences, you will be able to fish selectively for one species or another.

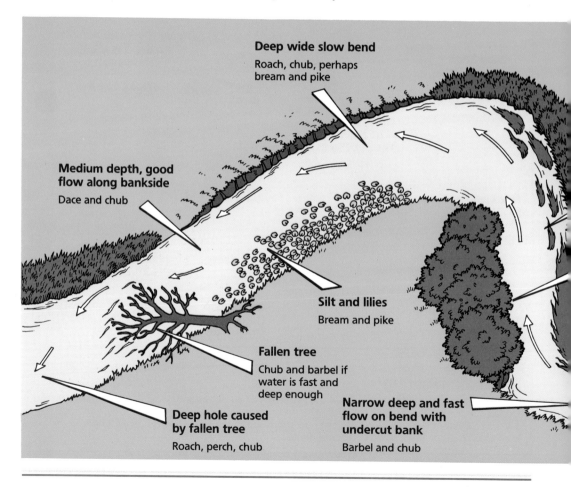

Deep wide slow bend
Roach, chub, perhaps bream and pike

Medium depth, good flow along bankside
Dace and chub

Silt and lilies
Bream and pike

Fallen tree
Chub and barbel if water is fast and deep enough

Deep hole caused by fallen tree
Roach, perch, chub

Narrow deep and fast flow on bend with undercut bank
Barbel and chub

Where to find the fish . . .

Barbel	Deep, fast areas, especially narrow areas, deep depressions on the river bed and deep bends with undercut banks.
Chub	Similar to barbel but don't mind shallower spots or slightly slacker water, though they do love cover over their heads.
Roach, bream	Slacker swims, especially deep, slow bends and eddies. At the back end of the season they like the areas just above weir pools.
Pike	Anywhere there are small fish.

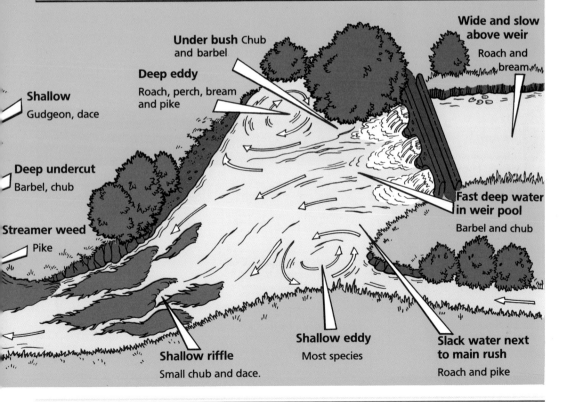

Wide and slow above weir
Roach and bream

Under bush Chub and barbel

Deep eddy
Roach, perch, bream and pike

Shallow
Gudgeon, dace

Deep undercut
Barbel, chub

Streamer weed
Pike

Fast deep water in weir pool
Barbel and chub

Shallow riffle
Small chub and dace.

Shallow eddy
Most species

Slack water next to main rush
Roach and pike

Float Fishing Methods

The main intention is to present a bait trotted down the stream at a controlled speed to match the flow on the river bed. This is roughly one-third slower than the surface flow.

Running water floats

These are the basic floats you'll need for float fishing in rivers.

Stick float

The most precise way of trotting downstream and ideal for dace, chub and roach.

Avon

Very versatile trotting float ideal for beginners.

Balsa

For carrying bigger baits, or for use in fast water.

Stick float rig

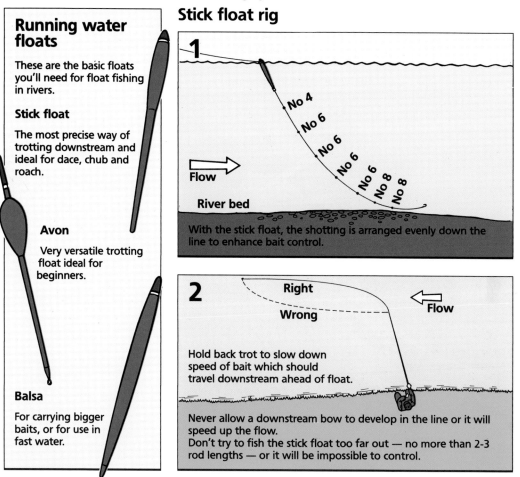

1

No 4
No 6
No 6
No 6
No 6
No 8
No 8

Flow

River bed

With the stick float, the shotting is arranged evenly down the line to enhance bait control.

2

Right

Wrong

Flow

Hold back trot to slow down speed of bait which should travel downstream ahead of float.

Never allow a downstream bow to develop in the line or it will speed up the flow.
Don't try to fish the stick float too far out — no more than 2-3 rod lengths — or it will be impossible to control.

Wagglers

In slower swims where the fish are further out, a stick float will be impossible to cast or control. A straight waggler is the only option here. Presentation will be less precise, but it is nevertheless an excellent method which will often take fish with the bait on the drop.

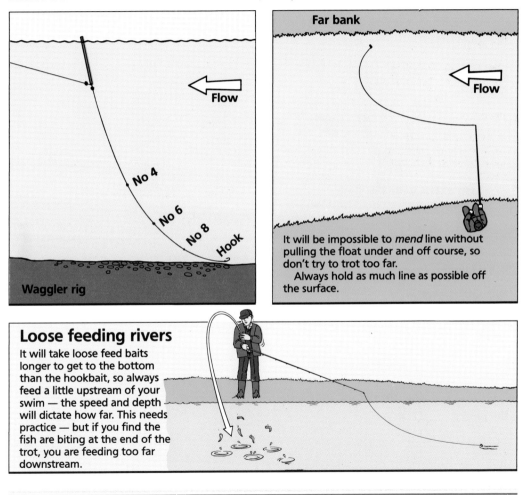

Flow

No 4

No 6

No 8

Hook

Waggler rig

Far bank

Flow

It will be impossible to *mend* line without pulling the float under and off course, so don't try to trot too far.

Always hold as much line as possible off the surface.

Loose feeding rivers

It will take loose feed baits longer to get to the bottom than the hookbait, so always feed a little upstream of your swim — the speed and depth will dictate how far. This needs practice — but if you find the fish are biting at the end of the trot, you are feeding too far downstream.

Legering Methods
Basic legering rigs for river fishing
Rolling legers can be rolled right under downstream overhanging bushes where accurate casting would be virtually impossible.

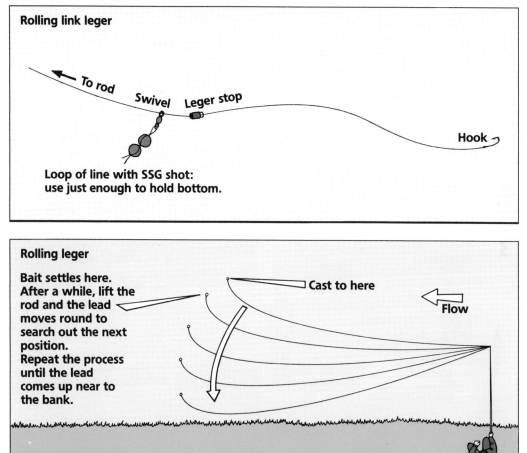

Rolling link leger

To rod   Swivel   Leger stop

Hook

Loop of line with SSG shot:
use just enough to hold bottom.

Rolling leger

Bait settles here.
After a while, lift the
rod and the lead
moves round to
search out the next
position.
Repeat the process
until the lead
comes up near to
the bank.

Cast to here

Flow

Feeder fishing

Here the *swimfeeder* empties your baits into one spot. Recast accurately and regularly to build up the *swim*. Keep as much line out of the water as possible otherwise the flow will drag the feeder out of the swim.

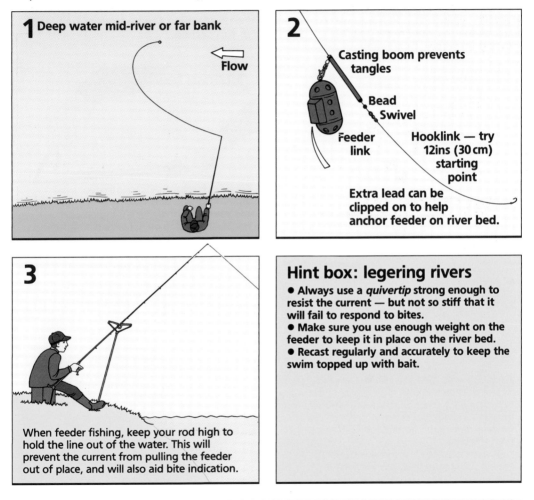

1 Deep water mid-river or far bank

Flow

2

Casting boom prevents tangles

Bead
Swivel

Feeder link

Hooklink — try 12ins (30 cm) starting point

Extra lead can be clipped on to help anchor feeder on river bed.

3

When feeder fishing, keep your rod high to hold the line out of the water. This will prevent the current from pulling the feeder out of place, and will also aid bite indication.

Hint box: legering rivers

● Always use a *quivertip* strong enough to resist the current — but not so stiff that it will fail to respond to bites.
● Make sure you use enough weight on the feeder to keep it in place on the river bed.
● Recast regularly and accurately to keep the swim topped up with bait.

BAITS

Types of Bait

Having decided where and what to fish, and which tackle to use, you have one more choice to make — which bait will best attract the fish? Almost anything can be used as bait, and some of the best and most popular are described in this section.

Bait is presented in three main ways.

1 Hookbaits

How you bait your hook, and what with, is a major factor in your success rate. The best hookbaits are detailed on the following pages.

2 Loose feeding

This is as it sounds — you introduce small amounts of bait direct to the swim. You can use the same baits you're using on your hooks. It's hard to get loose feed any distance, but using a *catapult* can help you reach further into the swim.

3 Groundbait

A mixture used to attract fish to the swim, groundbait consists of soft balls designed to disintegrate in the water. The basic ingredients for groundbait are brown bread crumbs and water mixed to a paste, but other ingredients are often added. Because of its form, groundbait can obviously be thrown further from the bank.

As with loose feed, the idea is to get fish to congregate and feed in the area so that they then fall for your hook bait.

Hint box: feeding the swim

- Don't overdo it — a common fault is to overfeed.
- Keep the fish competing for food.
- A little at a time is the best advice.
- If a small amount of groundbait gets the fish biting, add a little more.
- If you *don't* get any bites, there's no point adding more and more groundbait.

Maggot Baits

The most popular baits of all and good for most species except pike.

	Notes	**How to use**	**Hook**
Maggots	• You can use maggots singly or in pairs or multiples. • Dyed maggots in different colours are available. • Buy from the tackle shop by the pint. Make sure they are fresh and cleaned in maize meal. • Keep maggots in the fridge.	Mount a single maggot through the tiny flap of skin at the blunt end so it wriggles away from the point of the hook.	24-18 for single maggots. 18-14 for double maggots. 14-12 for multiples. Use a forged hook when you're fishing for larger species.
Squatts	• Larvae of the common housefly. • Keep squatts in sand. • Don't keep well in the fridge. • Very light, so good if you want a slow-sinking hookbait. • Useful to mix with groundbait.	Mainly used as loose feed or in groundbait.	24-22 for singles. 20 for doubles.
Casters	• A caster is a maggot chrysalis in its earliest stages — before it floats. • Good as loose feed, in groundbait or as a hookbait and often attracts larger fish. • Buy the day before you go fishing and keep them in the fridge — they won't keep long. • On the bank, keep fresh in water.	Bury the hook inside the caster, or hook as for a maggot.	18-14.

Worm Baits

Particularly good for catching larger specimens, especially in winter flood conditions.

	Notes	**How to use**	**Hook**
Lobworm	• The largest worm. • Can be collected off the lawn at night. • Will keep well if left in cool, damp moss or damp paper. • You can use the whole worm or just the head.	Hook the worm once, through the middle, so it can wriggle.	12 for head only. 8-6 for whole worm, forged.
Redworm	• Find these in well rotted manure — turn over the bottom layers of your compost heap. • Dark red and smaller than lobworm. • Keep as for lobworm.	As for lobworm.	14-12 for single. 10-8 for bunches.
Brandling	• Find these in ripe compost. • Smaller than redworm with red and yellow stripes. • Not as good as an all-round bait such as lobworm or redworm, but useful for perch. • Keep them in damp peat mixed with moss.	As for other worms.	16-12 for single. 12-10 for bunches.

Bread Baits

Bread makes cheap, versatile all-round baits.

	Notes	How to use	Hook
Bread crust	• Tinned loaf is best. • A good, buoyant bait useful for fishing on the surface for carp or on top of bottom weed. • Also useful for balancing other baits.	Cut off small squares with flake attached and hook as shown.	12-2 for large piece. 16-12 for small piece.
Bread flake	• Best made from white sliced — medium sliced for larger hook baits, thin sliced for smaller ones.	Pull off a piece large enough to cover the hook and leave the point exposed. Squeeze gently on round shank.	12-6 for large piece. 16-12 for small piece.

Miscellaneous and Special Baits

	Notes	How to use	Hook
Cheese paste	• Good all-round bait for larger fish. • Many cheeses — especially soft types — can be used. • Either mix with breadcrumb groundbait or use on its own, moulded to the required consistency.	Cheese paste hardens in water so mix as softly as possible. Mould onto hook — leave the point free.	14-6.

	Notes	How to use	Hook
Luncheon meat	● Mostly used in river fishing for barbel and chub, especially in flood conditions. ● Any brand will do.	Cut into cubes and push the hook through the middle so it comes out of the bottom with the point exposed.	12-6.
Trout pellets bait	● Known as TP paste. ● Buy from your tackle shop. ● Make a paste by adding boiling water and mashing until a firm consistency is achieved.	Can be hooked in two ways: ● Moulded round hook — make sure you leave the point free; ● Hair-rigged — mould around a bead tied to the end of the *hair*.	14-6.
Boilies	● Boilies are man-made, so-called because they are mixed, rolled into balls and then boiled. ● A wide variety of foodstuffs can be used e.g. milk proteins, fish meals, bird food, meat. ● Mix your basic ingredient to a paste with water or egg and boil in water. ● Ready made boilies in many flavours are available from tackle shops.	Boilies are usually used as a loose feed. As a hookbait, they are always used on a hair. Paste can be moulded onto a hook or hair bead (see Trout pellet).	12-16.

Seed Baits

	Notes	How to use	Hook
Hemp and tares	• These are used together — hemp is your loose feed and tares your hookbait. • You can also use hemp as a hookbait on its own. • Good all-round bait. • Buy dried hemp and cook it yourself — pre-soak then boil until it splits. • Tares need a bit more soaking and cooking.	Hemp: hook through the split. Tares: hook just under the skin.	18-16 Hemp. 16-14 Tares.
Sweetcorn	• Buy in tins rather than frozen — the fish like the higher sugar content! • Improves if removed from tin a day before use.	Hook singly or in multiples.	12 Single grain. 12-6 Multiples.

Hint box: hookbaits
• Using something different will often catch the fish — so don't be afraid to experiment.
• Larger species (or large-sized specimens) can consume far larger quantities of bait than smaller fish, so bait accordingly. While a $\frac{1}{2}$ pint (300ml) of bait may last all day for small fish, larger ones may eat ten times as much.
• Baits can be used in combination on the same hook (otherwise known as cocktails).
• Good combinations include bread and maggots, worms and casters.

Glossary

ANTI-REVERSE LEVER Lever on the reel which, when in the 'on' position, ensures that the handle only turns one way.

BALE ARM The pick-up for the line on the reel.

BARBEL (or BARBULE) Sensory appendage which grows from the mouth of some fish.

BOBBIN Bite indicator used when legering.

BOILIES Balls of man-made paste bait made with egg and boiled hard; available ready-made.

BOLT RIG A Legering rig designed to make the fish bolt after picking up a bait.

BOMB Weight used in legering.

CATAPULT Item for propelling groundbait into the swim.

CLOSED-FACE reel A fixed-spool REEL in which the spool is encased.

COARSE FISH Freshwater fish which are not classed as game, i.e. all species except salmon family.

CRUCIANS Members of the carp family.

DISGORGER Tool for retrieving deeply set hooks from fish.

DOT THE FLOAT To weight the float down so that just the tip is showing above water.

EDDY Whirling water, found at the edge of a current or where two streams meet.

ELECTRIC BITE INDICATOR Electronic device which gives an audible indication of a bite when legering.

FEEDER FISHING see swimfeeder.

FLOAT FISHING Fishing method using a float both to present the bait at the required depth and to indicate bites.

FLOATER A bait which floats on the surface.

GROUNDBAIT Feed introduced to a swim to attract and hold fish there.

HAIR RIG A rig which presents the bait separate from the hook.

HOOKBAIT Any bait mounted on the hook.

HOOKLINK Length of line on which hook is tied.

HYBRID The offspring produced by the crossbreeding of two similar species.

LATERAL LINE A series of sensory organs along the flanks of a fish.

LAYING ON A float-fishing method in which the bait is laid on the bottom.

LEGERING Method of fishing where the bait is presented on the bottom using a weight and no float.

MATCH ANGLING Competitive fishing in which the total weight of the fish caught determines the winner or winning team. See pleasure angling, specimen angling.

MEND Straightening the line between the rod tip and float.

MONKEY CLIMBER Bite indicator for stillwater leger.

MONO-FILAMENT Synthetic fish line consisting of a single strand.

PINKIES Larvae of the greenbottle fly, a bait similar to squatts.

PLAYING Controlling and reeling in a fish once hooked.

PLEASURE ANGLING Fishing purely for pleasure.

PLUMMET Weight attached to the end of a line and cast to determine the depth of a swim.

PUMPING Tactic used to retrieve line when playing a fish.

QUIVERTIP A sensitive extension to a Legering rod which indicates bites.

RIG Collective term for the arrangement of terminal tackle.

RINGS Rings are positioned along the length of the rod to guide the line.

SHOTTING UP Attaching the split shot to the line.

SLIPPING CLUTCH Mechanism on a reel designed to give line automatically before breaking strain is reached.

SPECIMEN ANGLING Specialising in fishing for large specimens of any species.

SPLIT SHOT Small weights used to cock a float, so-called because they have a split in one half for attaching to the line.

SWIM The area of water being fished.

SWIMFEEDER A device, usually made of perforated plastic tubing, attached to the line near the hook to distribute groundbait in a swim when legering.

SWING TIP An extension to a legering rod which indicates bites.

TACKLE Collective term for all the items of equipment used in angling.

TERMINAL TACKLE Term used to describe the tackle from the float to the hook (float fishing), or the lead to the hook (legering).

TIP RING The ring at the tip, or end, of the rod.

TROTTING River float-fishing method in which the bait is repeatedly worked downstream, then retrieved and allowed to drift again.

WEIR An obstruction built across a river to hold back water.